THE CHRISTMAS COLLECTION

25 DAYS TO SLOW DOWN AND SAVOR THE SEASON

ANDREW KING

Copyright © 2025 by Andrew King
All rights reserved.

No part of this book may be reproduced, stored in a retrieval system, or transmitted in any form or by any means—electronic, mechanical, photocopying, recording, or otherwise—without prior written permission of the author, except for brief quotations used in reviews or articles.

Title: The Christmas Collection
Author: Andrew King

Scripture quotations, unless otherwise noted, are from the Holy Bible, New International Version®, NIV®.
Copyright © 1973, 1978, 1984, 2011 by Biblica, Inc.™
Used by permission. All rights reserved worldwide.
First Edition, 2025

ISBN: 979-8-9935546-0-0
Cover Design: Bryson Breakey

Printed in the United States of America

INTRODUCTION

Friends and Family,

Merry Christmas! I'm so glad you're joining me on this 25-day journey through the Christmas story. If you're like me, you love this time of year. From twinkling lights on the house to singing carols to the chill in the Georgia air—I'm here for all of it. The whole world, it seems, gets caught up in the Christmas season.

But in the same breath, the pace of life this time of year can be exhausting. As the famous carol says, "the weary world rejoices." Yet so often, we never seem to get past the weary part. Can you relate? Me too.

And that's why I wrote this devotional. It's meant to be an intentional moment each day to slow down and focus on the true heart of Christmas—the birth of Jesus, the Son of the Living God. The One who came to take away the sins of the world. The One who makes our crooked paths straight. The One who brings eternal peace.

He first entered the world as a baby. Born in Bethlehem. To real parents. Announced by angels. Visited by shepherds. This is why we celebrate. More importantly, this is who we celebrate.

Before you begin the daily devotionals, I want to invite you to read the Christmas story straight from Scripture. Over the next 25 days, we'll reflect on different moments from this miraculous event—but there's something powerful about experiencing the full story in one sitting. As you read the Gospel accounts from Matthew and Luke, take a deep breath. Picture the scenes. Hear the angels' song. Imagine the night sky over Bethlehem. Allow yourself to experience the wonder of Jesus' birth.

Return to these passages as often as you'd like throughout this devotional. My hope is that they anchor your heart in the beauty and simplicity of the greatest story ever told.

My invitation to you is simple: join me in slowing down this season. Let's fix our hearts and minds on the true meaning of Christmas. It's all about Jesus.

I'm thankful for you, and thankful to experience a little bit of Christmas with you this year.

With joy,

Andy

Matthew 1:18-25 NIV

[18] This is how the birth of Jesus the Messiah came about: His mother Mary was pledged to be married to Joseph, but before they came together, she was found to be pregnant through the Holy Spirit. [19] Because Joseph her husband was faithful to the law, and yet did not want to expose her to public disgrace, he had in mind to divorce her quietly. [20] But after he had considered this, an angel of the Lord appeared to him in a dream and said, "Joseph son of David, do not be afraid to take Mary home as your wife, because what is conceived in her is from the Holy Spirit. [21] She will give birth to a son, and you are to give him the name Jesus, because he will save his people from their sins." [22] All this took place to fulfill what the Lord had said through the prophet: [23] "The virgin will conceive and give birth to a son, and they will call him Immanuel" (which means "God with us"). [24] When Joseph woke up, he did what the angel of the Lord had commanded him and took Mary home as his wife. [25] But he did not consummate their marriage until she gave birth to a son. And he gave him the name Jesus.

Luke 1:26-56 NIV

[26] In the sixth month of Elizabeth's pregnancy, God sent the angel Gabriel to Nazareth, a town in Galilee, [27] to a virgin pledged to be married to a man named Joseph, a descendant of David. The virgin's name was Mary. [28] The angel went to her and said, "Greetings, you who are highly favored! The Lord is with you."

[29] Mary was greatly troubled at his words and wondered what kind of greeting this might be. [30] But the angel said to her, "Do not be afraid, Mary; you have found favor with God. [31] You will conceive and give birth to a son,

and you are to call him Jesus. ³² He will be great and will be called the Son of the Most High. The Lord God will give him the throne of his father David, ³³ and he will reign over Jacob's descendants forever; his kingdom will never end."

³⁴ "How will this be," Mary asked the angel, "since I am a virgin?"

³⁵ The angel answered, "The Holy Spirit will come on you, and the power of the Most High will overshadow you. So the holy one to be born will be called[a] the Son of God. ³⁶ Even Elizabeth your relative is going to have a child in her old age, and she who was said to be unable to conceive is in her sixth month. ³⁷ For no word from God will ever fail."

³⁸ "I am the Lord's servant," Mary answered. "May your word to me be fulfilled." Then the angel left her.

³⁹ At that time Mary got ready and hurried to a town in the hill country of Judea, ⁴⁰ where she entered Zechariah's home and greeted Elizabeth. ⁴¹ When Elizabeth heard Mary's greeting, the baby leaped in her womb, and Elizabeth was filled with the Holy Spirit. ⁴² In a loud voice she exclaimed: "Blessed are you among women, and blessed is the child you will bear! ⁴³ But why am I so favored, that the mother of my Lord should come to me? ⁴⁴ As soon as the sound of your greeting reached my ears, the baby in my womb leaped for joy. ⁴⁵ Blessed is she who has believed that the Lord would fulfill his promises to her!"

⁴⁶ And Mary said:

"My soul glorifies the Lord
⁴⁷ and my spirit rejoices in God my Savior,
⁴⁸ for he has been mindful
   of the humble state of his servant.
From now on all generations will call me blessed,
⁴⁹ for the Mighty One has done great things for me—
   holy is his name.
⁵⁰ His mercy extends to those who fear him,
   from generation to generation.
⁵¹ He has performed mighty deeds with his arm;
   he has scattered those who are proud in their inmost thoughts.
⁵² He has brought down rulers from their thrones
   but has lifted up the humble.
⁵³ He has filled the hungry with good things
   but has sent the rich away empty.
⁵⁴ He has helped his servant Israel,
   remembering to be merciful
⁵⁵ to Abraham and his descendants forever,
   just as he promised our ancestors."

⁵⁶ Mary stayed with Elizabeth for about three months and then returned home.

Luke 2:1-20 NIV

¹ In those days Caesar Augustus issued a decree that a census should be taken of the entire Roman world. ² (This was the first census that took place while Quirinius was governor of Syria.) ³ And everyone went to their own town to register.

⁴ So Joseph also went up from the town of Nazareth in Galilee to Judea, to Bethlehem the town of David, because he belonged to the house and line of David. ⁵ He went there to register with Mary, who was pledged to be married to him and was expecting a child. ⁶ While they were there, the time came for the baby to be born, ⁷ and she gave birth to her firstborn, a son. She wrapped him in cloths and placed him in a manger, because there was no guest room available for them.

⁸ And there were shepherds living out in the fields nearby, keeping watch over their flocks at night. ⁹ An angel of the Lord appeared to them, and the glory of the Lord shone around them, and they were terrified. ¹⁰ But the angel said to them, "Do not be afraid. I bring you good news that will cause great joy for all the people. ¹¹ Today in the town of David a Savior has been born to you; he is the Messiah, the Lord. ¹² This will be a sign to you: You will find a baby wrapped in cloths and lying in a manger."

¹³ Suddenly a great company of the heavenly host appeared with the angel, praising God and saying,

¹⁴ "Glory to God in the highest heaven,
 and on earth peace to those on whom his favor rests."

[15] When the angels had left them and gone into heaven, the shepherds said to one another, "Let's go to Bethlehem and see this thing that has happened, which the Lord has told us about."

[16] So they hurried off and found Mary and Joseph, and the baby, who was lying in the manger. [17] When they had seen him, they spread the word concerning what had been told them about this child, [18] and all who heard it were amazed at what the shepherds said to them. [19] But Mary treasured up all these things and pondered them in her heart. [20] The shepherds returned, glorifying and praising God for all the things they had heard and seen, which were just as they had been told.

DAY ONE
HOLY SCANDAL

Matthew 1:18 NIV *This is how the birth of Jesus the Messiah came about: His mother Mary was pledged to be married to Joseph, but before they came together, she was found to be pregnant through the Holy Spirit.*

The birth of Jesus was no accident. It wasn't a last-minute rescue plan or a sudden idea that came to God on a Sunday afternoon. It was a sacred moment, written into eternity and fulfilled in God's perfect timing.

Yet consider how the birth of Jesus "came about."

Mary, a young woman pledged to Joseph, suddenly found herself pregnant—not by her husband-to-be, but by the Holy Spirit. Who would ever believe her? The whispers would start immediately. Gossip in the marketplace. Raised eyebrows from neighbors. Joseph, confused and heartbroken, quietly weighing what to do. This was the backdrop for the most important birth in history!

Yet this was God's plan.

It wasn't neat, polished, or easily explained. It was messy. Misunderstood. Full of tension and risk. And still, it was divinely ordained.

Have you ever felt that way—confused about what God is doing in your life? Unsure why certain things are unfolding the way they are? You're in good company. Mary walked that road before you.

The first Christmas reminds us that even when we can't see the full picture, God is faithfully at work. His ways are often mysterious. His timing rarely looks like ours. But His plans are never random. He is always weaving redemption—even through chaos and uncertainty.

But just because it's difficult doesn't mean God isn't in it.

The question isn't whether we understand His plan.

The question is whether we will trust Him anyway.

REFLECTION

When have you felt confused or uncertain about God's work in your life?

. . . .
. . . .
. . . .

How does Mary's story encourage you to trust Him?

. . . .
. . . .
. . . .

What would it look like for you to surrender your uncertainties and rest in His plan today?

. . . .
. . . .
. . . .

PRAYER

Father, thank You that Your ways are higher than mine. Even when life feels unclear, I believe You are at work. Give me courage to trust You when I don't have the answers. Just as You worked through Mary's story, I know You are working in mine. Amen.

DAY TWO
LEAD WITH MERCY

Matthew 1:19 NIV *"Because Joseph her husband was faithful to the law, and yet did not want to expose her to public disgrace, he had in mind to divorce her quietly."*

We don't know much about Joseph, yet the fact that God chose him to raise His Son speaks volumes. Joseph wasn't known as a charismatic leader, a wealthy merchant, or an extraordinary athlete. What marked him was something far greater: character.

Scripture tells us Joseph was faithful to the law, yet unwilling to disgrace Mary. As a devout, Torah-observant man, he knew what the law required. In first-century Jewish culture, unfaithfulness during betrothal was considered adultery—a serious offense with devastating consequences. A strict, legal response could have destroyed Mary's life and reputation forever.

But Joseph's faithfulness wasn't cold or legalistic. His devotion to God's Word was infused with mercy. He searched for a way to uphold righteousness without crushing Mary beneath the weight of shame. He looked for a quiet solution, one that reflected both his integrity and his compassion.

Joseph's actions show us that true obedience to God is never divorced from love. His quiet strength reminds us that faithfulness to God's commands must always be expressed through kindness.

Joseph points us to the greatness of Jesus—who fulfilled the law perfectly, yet offered mercy to sinners like us.

Joseph was a man of both conviction and compassion. He teaches us that when faced with the failures of others, mercy should lead the way.

REFLECTION

When you face difficult situations, do you allow mercy to guide your response?

. . . .
. . . .
. . . .

How do you balance faithfulness to God's truth with compassion for people?

. . . .
. . . .
. . . .

What would it look like for you to reflect Joseph's blend of righteousness and kindness today?

. . . .
. . . .
. . . .

PRAYER

Father, thank You for Joseph's example of faithful compassion. Help me to walk in Your truth with a heart full of mercy. When I face difficult situations, give me the wisdom to respond with both conviction and kindness. May my life point others to the mercy and righteousness of Jesus. Amen.

DAY THREE
YOU ARE ROYALTY

Matthew 1:20 NIV *But after he had considered this, an angel of the Lord appeared to him in a dream and said, "Joseph son of David, do not be afraid to take Mary home as your wife, because what is conceived in her is from the Holy Spirit.*

Joseph had already made up his mind. The relationship was over. Plans ended. Dreams crushed.

But then...an angel in a dream.

"Joseph son of David, do not be afraid..."

The angel isn't just telling a random guy not to fear—he's speaking to a man in the Davidic line who will raise the Messiah. God had promised David that one of his descendants would reign forever (2 Samuel 7:12-16). By calling Joseph "son of David," the angel reminds him—and us— that Joseph is part of that covenant line.

Joseph may have felt small and unqualified for what the angel was asking. He's a carpenter in a small town, not a palace ruler. But the angel's words serve as a powerful reminder:

You come from a royal line. You are part of God's rescue story. You have a part to play.

Joseph wasn't an accidental participant. He's in the story because God placed him there. That same truth applies to us. Before God calls us to act in faith, He reminds us of our identity.

Paul writes in Romans 8:16–17: *The Spirit himself testifies with our spirit that we are God's children. Now if we are children, then we are heirs—heirs of God and co-heirs with Christ...*

Just as Joseph's role in God's plan was anchored in his identity as a son of David, our courage to follow God comes from knowing we are sons and daughters of the King. We are not spiritual outsiders or nameless servants—we are heirs of God.

When you remember who you belong to, fear begins to lose its grip. God doesn't just call you to hard things; He reminds you that you have a royal identity and His Spirit living in you to accomplish them.

REFLECTION

Where in your life is fear holding you back from obedience?

. . . .
. . . .
. . . .

How might remembering your identity as an heir of God change the way you step forward today?

. . . .
. . . .
. . . .

PRAYER

Father, thank You that I am Your child and a co-heir with Christ. Remind me of who I am in You when fear rises up. Give me courage to walk in obedience, knowing that You have already secured my place in Your family and Your plan. Amen.

DAY FOUR
HIS NAME IS JESUS

Matthew 1:21 NIV *She will give birth to a son, and you are to give him the name Jesus, because he will save his people from their sins.*

Names matter. In some cultures, names reflect what is fashionable in the moment. In others, they declare identity and purpose, pointing to what a child is destined to accomplish.

So what about the name Jesus?

It was a common boy's name at the time, the Hebrew form being Joshua. Joshua was the leader who brought Israel into the promised land after Moses' death. In the same way, Jesus would finish what the law of Moses could never complete—bringing true freedom. Not freedom from Egypt. Not freedom from Roman rule. But freedom from the deepest bondage of all: sin.

Throughout Scripture, God gives names that reveal mission and meaning: Ishmael. Isaac. Solomon. John the Baptist. Each carried a divine purpose attached to their identity. Their names were more than labels; they were declarations of destiny.

The same is true with Jesus. His very name means "The Lord saves." His mission was clear from the beginning—to rescue His people from their sins.

And here's the good news: the same God who gave Jesus His name also knows yours. Long before you took your first breath, He saw your story. He knows your strengths and weaknesses. He understands the chapters still unwritten. Your identity isn't defined by culture, your past, or even your successes. It is defined by the One who created you and calls you His own.

The God who named and commissioned His people throughout history is still speaking identity and purpose over your life today. You can trust Him with your story.

REFLECTION

Do you find your truest identity in what God says about you—or in what culture or others say?

. . . .
. . . .
. . . .

How does Jesus' name remind you of your need for Him as Savior?

. . . .
. . . .
. . . .

What would it look like to trust God with your identity and your future today?

. . . .

. . . .

. . . .

PRAYER

Lord, thank You for knowing me fully and calling me by name. Help me to live in the identity You have given me, not the one the world tries to impose. I trust the story You are writing for my life. Give me courage to walk in the purpose You set for me from the beginning. Amen.

DAY FIVE
GOD WITH YOU

Matthew 1:22-23 NIV *All this took place to fulfill what the Lord had said through the prophet: 'The virgin will conceive and give birth to a son, and they will call him Immanuel' (which means 'God with us').*

The birth of Jesus wasn't a sudden idea. It had been foretold centuries earlier.

Nearly 750 years before Christ, Judah faced threats from neighboring nations. Fear gripped King Ahaz, and instead of trusting God, he considered a foreign alliance for protection. But God sent the prophet Isaiah with a message of hope: before the crisis could overtake them, a child would be born. This baby would be a living sign that God was present with His people and that they could place their trust in Him rather than in human alliances.

While Isaiah's prophecy had immediate meaning in his day, Matthew highlights its ultimate fulfillment in Jesus. This child wasn't just a sign of God's presence—He was God's presence. Immanuel. God with us.

And this time, the deliverance wouldn't be temporary. It wouldn't just rescue a nation from political enemies. Jesus came to bring eternal freedom, once and for all, from sin and death.

Think about it: more than seven centuries passed between

Isaiah's prophecy and the birth of Jesus. Kingdoms rose and fell. Generations lived and died. Yet God's Word endured. His promises were not forgotten. And when the time was right, they came true in ways more wonderful than anyone could have imagined.

That same truth holds for us today. What God speaks, He will accomplish. His Word outlasts nations, crises, and lifetimes. And His promise to be with you remains unshakable.

REFLECTION

Are there promises from God's Word you've been waiting on that feel delayed?

. . . .
. . . .
. . . .

How does Jesus as Immanuel encourage you to trust God's timing?

. . . .
. . . .
. . . .

When has God surprised you by fulfilling His promises in unexpected ways?

. . . .

. . . .

. . . .

PRAYER

Lord, You are faithful through every generation. Thank You that Your promises never expire and that Your timing is always perfect. Help me to trust You when I cannot see the full picture. Anchor my hope in You alone, knowing kingdoms rise and fall, but Your Word endures forever. Amen.

DAY SIX
DO IT AFRAID

Matthew 1:24 NIV *When Joseph woke up, he did what the angel of the Lord had commanded him and took Mary home as his wife.*

Joseph had made up his mind to quietly divorce Mary. Then everything changed. An angel appeared in a dream and gave him a clear command: take Mary as your wife.

When Joseph woke up, he obeyed.

That sounds simple—but Joseph was still human. Surely he felt fear. Surely he had questions. Surely he wondered how this would all play out. Yet Joseph didn't wait for full understanding before obeying. He trusted God and did what was commanded—even if it meant doing it afraid.

We often assume that obedience and fear are opposites. That obedience should feel easy, or that it will only come once we fully understand God's plan. But the truth is, understanding can wait. Obedience cannot.

Life is full of moments where God calls us to move forward without all the answers. Moving to a new city. Starting a new job. Sharing your faith with a friend. Confronting sin in your life. Extending forgiveness. Giving generously. Launching a Bible study. None of these come with guarantees of how things will turn out. But each one requires obedience.

Rarely do faithful obedience and perfect clarity go hand in hand. More often, God calls us to trust Him in the unknown. To follow Him even when fear whispers. To step forward even when the path isn't clear.

Joseph's story reminds us that courage isn't the absence of fear—it's the choice to obey God in spite of it. Sometimes obedience looks like doing it afraid.

REFLECTION

Where is fear holding you back from obeying God?

How might Joseph's example encourage you to trust God without waiting for full clarity?

What step of faith is God asking you to take right now?

PRAYER

Lord, thank You for reminding me that obedience doesn't require perfect understanding. Give me courage to follow You even when I feel afraid. Help me to trust that Your ways are good and that You are with me every step of the way. Amen.

DAY SEVEN
GOD'S GLORY IN THE PLACES WE OVERLOOK

Luke 1:26-27 NIV *In the sixth month of Elizabeth's pregnancy, God sent the angel Gabriel to Nazareth, a town in Galilee, to a virgin pledged to be married to a man named Joseph, a descendant of David. The virgin's name was Mary.*

When we imagine the grand arrival of the Son of God, we might picture palaces, city gates, or bustling centers of power. But Luke tells us that the angel Gabriel didn't go to Jerusalem—the religious capital. He didn't go to Rome—the political powerhouse. Instead, he went to Nazareth.

Nazareth was a small, out-of-the-way village. So insignificant that people scoffed at it. Nathanael summed up the common opinion in John 1:46: "Can anything good come from there?" And yet, that's where God chose to begin the story of Jesus' arrival.

Think about it: all of creation had been waiting for the Messiah, the fulfillment of God's redemptive plan stretching back to Eden. And where does the story turn? Not in the corridors of kings, but in a forgotten village. Not through a famous family, but through a humble young woman from Nazareth.

God's choice of Nazareth reminds us of a timeless truth: He delights in working through the unnoticed, the ordinary, and the overlooked. He writes world-changing stories from places most people would pass by without a thought.

So if you feel hidden or overlooked, take heart. God knows exactly where you are. He isn't limited by your background, your résumé, or your address. In fact, He specializes in turning small beginnings into eternal impact.

--- **REFLECTION** ---

Where in your life do you feel small or overlooked?

. . . .
. . . .
. . . .

How might God want to use those very places for extraordinary purposes?

. . . .
. . . .
. . . .

What does Nazareth teach you about the way God works in unexpected ways?

. . . .
. . . .
. . . .

PRAYER

Lord, thank You that You see me even when I feel unseen. Thank You for choosing the unexpected to carry out Your greatest work. Help me to trust that where I am right now is not beyond Your reach or Your plan. Open my eyes to the opportunities in front of me, and give me faith to believe You can bring eternal impact from small beginnings. Use my life, Lord, for Your glory—no matter how hidden or humble the setting. Amen.

DAY EIGHT
FAVORED BY GOD

Luke 1:28 NIV *The angel went to her and said, 'Greetings, you who are highly favored! The Lord is with you.*

Mary was the recipient of God's grace. Not because of her merit, but because of God's initiative.

This is important: the birth of Jesus, like all of God's wondrous works, was not the result of human planning or striving. His timing, His location, His choice of parents—all of it was an outpouring of divine favor. Mary was chosen, not because she earned the role, but because of God's kindness.

And she wasn't alone in this story of grace. Scripture is filled with examples:

- Noah found favor in the eyes of the Lord (Genesis 6:8).
- Moses found favor in God's sight (Exodus 33:17).
- Esther found favor in the eyes of the king (Esther 2:15–17).
- David. Daniel. Gideon. Hannah.

All of them were favored by God—not through flawless records or personal achievements, but through His goodness and faithfulness.

Paul echoes this truth in Ephesians: God's favor is His undeserved kindness poured out on us because of who He is, not what we've done. Grace is not a paycheck for performance. It is a gift freely given.

None of us can earn it.

All of us desperately need it.

And the same God who favored Mary, Noah, and Moses has set His favor on you in Christ—to save you, sustain you, and send you.

When you walk in that truth, your life becomes a testimony of His goodness and faithfulness.

REFLECTION

Do you think of God's favor as something to achieve—or something already given to you in Christ?

. . . .
. . . .
. . . .

How might your outlook change if you fully believed you are living under God's grace today?

. . . .
. . . .
. . . .

In what ways could you extend that same grace to others?

PRAYER

Lord, thank You that Your favor rests on me because of Jesus. Help me to walk in the joy and humility of knowing I am chosen, loved, and sent by You. Let my life reflect Your grace to others today. Amen.

DAY NINE
WHEN YOU FEEL TROUBLED

Luke 1:29 NIV *Mary was greatly troubled at his words and wondered what kind of greeting this might be.*

"Greatly troubled."

Not the reaction we usually associate with angels, divine favor, or God's plans coming to life. But that's exactly how Mary felt—shaken and unsettled.

The Greek word translated "greatly troubled" (diatarassō) goes beyond simple confusion. It carries the weight of being disturbed, deeply agitated, even shaken in one's thoughts. Mary wasn't primarily troubled by the angel's presence—though that would have been enough to rattle anyone. What disturbed her most was the greeting itself.

She knew that God's favor often came with responsibility. His call wasn't simply a compliment; it was a commission. Mary likely realized in that moment that God had something significant for her to do, and the weight of it pressed heavily on her.

It's no wonder she felt troubled—her thoughts racing, her mind restless, her spirit anxious. She had been chosen to be the mother of the Messiah. The entire world was about to change, and she was at the center of it.

And isn't that how we often feel? When the future feels uncertain. When God's direction seems overwhelming. When His call feels more like pressure than peace.

But Mary's story reminds us of something vital: being troubled doesn't mean being faithless. It means being human. And God doesn't abandon us in our troubled thoughts—He meets us there. He steadies restless hearts, calms anxious minds, and reminds us that His presence is with us every step of the way.

REFLECTION

Have you ever felt troubled by what God is doing in your life?

. . . .
. . . .
. . . .

What thoughts or fears keep circling in your mind?

. . . .
. . . .
. . . .

What would it look like to bring those honest struggles before Him today?

. . . .
. . . .
. . . .

PRAYER

Lord, You see my troubled thoughts and restless heart. Just like Mary, I don't always understand what You're doing, but I want to trust You anyway. Calm my mind, steady my spirit, and remind me that Your presence is with me—even when peace feels far away. Amen.

DAY TEN
TRUE GREATNESS

Luke 1:30-33 NIV *But the angel said to her, 'Do not be afraid, Mary; you have found favor with God. You will conceive and give birth to a son, and you are to call him Jesus. He will be great and will be called the Son of the Most High. The Lord God will give him the throne of his father David, and he will reign over Jacob's descendants forever; his kingdom will never end.'*

"He will be great."

It's every parent's dream to see their child excel. Just attend a high school game and listen to the proud voices in the stands. But Gabriel's announcement about Jesus wasn't about talent or skill. It was something far deeper.

In Scripture, the word "great" is most often used in connection with God Himself or with those appointed for His purposes. Abraham's name would be made great. Moses was regarded as great in Egypt. David was promised greatness through a royal line. In every case, greatness wasn't earned—it was granted.

And here Gabriel proclaims that Jesus will be great—not because of what He achieves, but because of who He is. His greatness is not measured by human standards of power, popularity, or success. It doesn't depend on comparison or competition. Jesus is greatness.

He is the Son of the Most High.
He carries authority over life, death, and sin.
He reigns on David's throne with an eternal kingdom.
He perfectly reveals God's character.

There is no one like Him.

Jesus wasn't simply great at something. He is greatness incarnate. And when we measure our lives by Him, our perspective shifts. We stop chasing greatness by the world's definition and rest in the greatness of Christ.

REFLECTION

Where are you tempted to define greatness by human standards—career, parenting, ministry, reputation?

. . . .
. . . .
. . . .

How does Jesus' identity as true greatness reshape your perspective?

. . . .
. . . .
. . . .

What area of your life needs to be surrendered to His eternal kingdom rather than your own success?

. . . .

. . . .

. . . .

PRAYER

Jesus, You are the standard of greatness—unmatched in power, love, and truth. Forgive me when I chase success or significance in the wrong ways. Teach me to rest in Your greatness, not my own. Help me to see that Your eternal kingdom is far greater than anything I could build for myself. Amen.

DAY ELEVEN
HONEST QUESTIONS

Luke 1:34 NIV *'How will this be,' Mary asked the angel, 'since I am a virgin?'*

Mary had questions.

She didn't scoff. She didn't argue. But she also didn't nod her head in blind agreement. She asked something real and reasonable: "How will this be?"

It's easy to imagine Mary's response as serene and unshakable, but this moment reveals something tender—Mary was trying to process the impossible news she had just heard. She wasn't doubting God's power; she simply couldn't grasp the how. Virgins don't have babies. What was promised to her defied biology, logic, and every expectation for her future.

Here's the beautiful part: God wasn't offended by her question.

The angel didn't silence or scold her. He answered. Mary's "how" was met with assurance. The angel explained that the Holy Spirit would come upon her, that the power of the Most High would overshadow her, and that what was impossible with man would be possible with God. Her honest question opened the door to a deeper glimpse of God's mysterious plan.

And the same is true for you.

You don't have to hide your questions from God. He isn't intimidated by your curiosity. He welcomes the seeking heart. Faith is not the absence of questions—it's choosing to trust God even as you bring those questions honestly before Him.

REFLECTION

What big questions are you carrying right now?

Are you hesitant to bring them to God?

How does Mary's example encourage you to approach Him with honesty and trust?

PRAYER

Father, thank You that You are not threatened by my questions. Thank You for meeting Mary with grace and clarity when she didn't understand. Help me bring my uncertainty to You with the same honesty. I don't need all the answers, but I do need Your presence. Teach me to trust You even when life doesn't add up. Amen.

DAY TWELVE
GOD BREAKS IN

Luke 1:35 NIV *The angel answered, 'The Holy Spirit will come on you, and the power of the Most High will overshadow you. So the holy one to be born will be called the Son of God.'*

From the opening verses of Genesis, we see the Spirit of God hovering over the chaos, bringing order and life into existence. In Exodus, God's presence overshadowed the tabernacle, filling it with His glory. And now, in Luke 1, the Spirit descends once more—this time upon a young woman named Mary. Through her, a new creation enters the world: Jesus, the Son of God.

The word overshadow is no accident.

It carries the language of divine presence—God drawing near. In this sacred moment, Mary becomes the vessel through which the Light of the World steps into human history.

This isn't just another miraculous birth.
This is God breaking in.
This is the holy becoming human.
But the beauty of Christmas is not only what happened then. It's what continues to happen now.

God still overshadows the empty and fills it with life. He still enters dark, hopeless places and declares, "Let there be light." And here's the breathtaking reality: the same Spirit that overshadowed Mary now dwells in every believer.

The miracle of Christmas isn't just that Jesus was born—it's that through Him we are reborn.

Jesus is God's new creation. And through Him, so are we.

REFLECTION

Where in your life do you feel empty, chaotic, or dark?

. . . .
. . . .
. . . .

How does Mary's story encourage you to invite God's Spirit into those places?

. . . .
. . . .
. . . .

What would it look like for you to say "yes" to becoming a new creation in Christ today?

. . . .
. . . .
. . . .

PRAYER

God, I open my heart to You today. Just as You overshadowed Mary and brought forth new life, would You fill me with Your Spirit and make me new? I believe Jesus is the Son of God, the Light of the World, and I receive His gift of salvation. Bring Your light into every dark and empty place in me. Make me a new creation—alive with Your presence, full of Your purpose, and walking in Your grace. Amen.

DAY THIRTEEN
HIS WORD NEVER FAILS

Luke 1:36-37 NIV *Even Elizabeth your relative is going to have a child in her old age, and she who was said to be unable to conceive is in her sixth month. For no word from God will ever fail.*

Elizabeth had been told she could never conceive.
Too old. Too late. Too impossible.

And yet—six months into her miraculous pregnancy, her growing baby declared a greater truth: nothing is impossible with God.

When Gabriel shared this news with Mary, it wasn't just an update—it was a testimony. A living reminder that God's promises are not wishful thinking. They are declarations of reality, even when we can't yet see them.

Gabriel was essentially saying: Look at Elizabeth. Everyone said it couldn't happen—but God said it would. And He was right. If God could bring life from barrenness, surely He could bring a Savior from a virgin's womb.

God's Word didn't fail Elizabeth.
It didn't fail Mary.
And it won't fail you.

But Gabriel's declaration reaches even further than these two women. It reverberates through history. Because the child Mary carried—Jesus—is the ultimate fulfillment of God's Word.

John's Gospel says it this way: "In the beginning was the Word... and the Word became flesh." (John 1:1, 14)

Jesus is not just a promise kept. He is the promise.
He is the living, breathing embodiment of God's faithfulness. He is the assurance that what God begins, He always brings to completion.

So when the waiting feels long, when the odds seem stacked against you, or when doubt whispers, remember: God's Word never fails. And Jesus is the proof.

REFLECTION

Where in your life do you need to be reminded that God's Word never fails?

. . . .
. . . .
. . . .

What feels too late, too far gone, or too impossible?

. . . .
. . . .
. . . .

Will you choose to trust today that God's promises still hold true for you?

. . . .

. . . .

. . . .

PRAYER

Faithful God, You always keep Your Word. Thank You for the testimony of Elizabeth and the miraculous birth of Jesus, the living Word. When I doubt, remind me that Your promises never fail. Strengthen my trust and help me to stand on what You have spoken—no matter what I see. Amen.

DAY FOURTEEN
I AM THE LORD'S SERVANT

Luke 1:38 NIV *'I am the Lord's servant,' Mary answered. 'May your word to me be fulfilled.' Then the angel left her.*

Mary's response to the angel reveals the posture of her heart. She didn't claim control, demand explanations, or hesitate with doubt. Instead, she declared her identity: a servant of the Lord. The word she used carried the sense of a handmaid—a personal attendant, even a slave. It was an intentional act of surrender.

What humility this young woman displayed!

No protest.
No disbelief.
No cynicism.

Only a willingness to trust God completely. If He spoke it, she believed it. If He willed it, she would obey.

It's easy to follow God when His instructions align with our plans, when obedience feels comfortable, or when faith doesn't cost us much. But true servanthood is tested in the moments when His will feels confusing, costly, or overwhelming. Mary's obedience would lead her through misunderstanding, hardship, and even sorrow—but nothing was stronger than her surrender.

In essence, Mary was saying: "There is nothing I won't do for the Lord. However difficult this may become, I belong to Him."

Her words are a timeless example for us. Servanthood isn't about partial obedience or selective trust. It's about wholehearted surrender, even when the path ahead is unclear.

REFLECTION

Is your heart truly surrendered to God's will?

. . . .
. . . .
. . . .

What areas of your life are easy to yield to Him—and where do you struggle to obey?

. . . .
. . . .
. . . .

What step of trust might He be inviting you to take today?

. . . .
. . . .
. . . .

PRAYER

Father, give me the heart of a servant. Teach me to surrender my plans, my comfort, and my control to You. Help me obey You fully, even when I don't understand the outcome. Like Mary, may I trust Your Word and walk in faithful obedience, confident that Your will is always good. Amen.

DAY FIFTEEN
THE GREAT REVERSAL

Luke 1:44-45 NIV *As soon as the sound of your greeting reached my ears, the baby in my womb leaped for joy. Blessed is she who has believed that the Lord would fulfill his promises to her!*

Jacob over Esau.
Joseph over his brothers.
David, the youngest son, chosen as king.

God's story has always been marked by reversals. And here, once again, the pattern continues.

Mary—a teenage virgin—is honored by Elizabeth, the wife of a respected priest. Jesus—the younger by six months—is celebrated by John, who should have held precedence by cultural norms. Yet still in the womb, John leaps for joy, acknowledging Jesus' lordship before either of them has taken a breath. The forerunner bows before the Messiah in a moment of Spirit-filled joy.

It's unprecedented—and a powerful reminder that God's kingdom does not follow the world's rules. It turns them upside down.
Normally, the Spirit of God came upon prophets, priests, or kings at defining moments of leadership. Here, the Spirit moves through an unborn child. And those often pushed to the margins—women and babies—are the very first to bear witness to the Messiah's arrival.

Even more, notice who speaks blessing. Not Zechariah, the patriarch of the house, who remains silent in his unbelief. It is Elizabeth who declares blessing over Mary, affirming her faith and God's promise.

What a series of reversals!

This is the heart of Christmas: God's kingdom breaking in through the unexpected, elevating the humble, and working through weakness to display His power. And He still delights in turning our assumptions upside down today.

REFLECTION

Where have you seen God overturn expectations in your life?

. . . .
. . . .
. . . .

How might the Spirit be inviting you to embrace His "great reversals" right now?

. . . .
. . . .
. . . .

Are you willing to let God write the story differently than you would have written it yourself?

. . . .

. . . .

. . . .

PRAYER

Father, thank You for showing me that Your ways are higher than mine. Help me trust You when life feels upside down. Keep me humble, open, and ready for the reversals You bring, knowing You are always faithful and perfectly good. Amen.

DAY SIXTEEN
MERCY AND JUSTICE

Luke 1:51–54 NIV *He has performed mighty deeds with his arm; he has scattered those who are proud in their inmost thoughts. He has brought down rulers from their thrones but has lifted up the humble. He has filled the hungry with good things but has sent the rich away empty. He has helped his servant Israel, remembering to be merciful...*

Mary's song—known as the Magnificat—is both a hymn of joy and a bold proclamation. She rejoices not only in what God has done for her personally but also in what He is doing for His people across generations.

Her words remind us that God is not passive. He acts. He scatters the proud. He dethrones rulers. He sends the self-sufficient rich away empty. Yet He lifts the humble. He fills the hungry. He remembers mercy.

At first, judgment may seem like a strange theme for a song of celebration. But for Mary—a poor, unnoticed teenage girl—this was very good news. Judgment meant God saw her. It meant the forgotten and oppressed were not overlooked. It meant His mighty arm was stretching out to set the world right.

In the Magnificat, mercy and justice are woven together. God's mercy cannot lift up the lowly without also bringing down the proud. His justice cannot scatter the arrogant without at the same time providing for the humble. Mary rejoices because she knows the Mighty One—the God of Abraham, Isaac, and Jacob—is keeping His covenant. His holiness is not empty talk; it is powerful, redemptive action.

The Christmas story is not sentimental. It is the declaration that God has come to deal with sin, pride, and injustice. Mary's joy is not shallow—it is rooted in the hope that God is making all things new.

REFLECTION

Where do you need to be reminded that God sees injustice and will act?

. . . .
. . . .
. . . .

What step can you take to reflect His mercy and justice to others?

. . . .
. . . .
. . . .

How does Mary's song help you celebrate both mercy and justice at once?

. . . .

. . . .

. . . .

PRAYER

Lord Almighty, thank You for being both merciful and just. I praise You for lifting the humble, satisfying the hungry, and remembering the forgotten. Help me to trust that You are at work, and shape me to love others like You do. Let my life echo Mary's song—rejoicing in Your mercy and justice. Amen.

DAY SEVENTEEN
REAL FAITH IN REAL LIFE

Luke 2:1-3 NIV *In those days Caesar Augustus issued a decree that a census should be taken of the entire Roman world. (This was the first census that took place while Quirinius was governor of Syria.) And everyone went to their own town to register.*

Quirinius. Caesar Augustus. Syria. The Roman Empire.

These aren't throwaway details—they are reminders that the story of Jesus didn't unfold in a mythical land or a once-upon-a-time fantasy. The Christmas story is anchored in real time, real people, and real places.

This wasn't "once upon a time." It was "in those days."

Historians outside the Bible reference Caesar Augustus and Quirinius, confirming that Luke's account took place during a verifiable moment in world history. It's Luke's way of saying: this really happened.

God stepped into actual time and space. Into a world ruled by an emperor. Into a political system that ignored Him. Into a culture marked by tension and division.
And He still does.

That's the wonder of Christmas. It's not just that Jesus came—it's that He came here. To earth. To a messy, complicated world filled with power plays, revolutions, and bureaucratic decrees.

God doesn't wait for perfect conditions to keep His promises. He moves right in the middle of the chaos, the ordinary, and the unexpected.

If you can trust Luke's historical details, you can trust the rest of the story too. That Jesus was born of a virgin. That He is the Savior. That God's Word is reliable from beginning to end.

If He was faithful then won't He be faithful now?

REFLECTION

How does the historical grounding of the Christmas story strengthen your confidence in Scripture?

. . . .
. . . .
. . . .

Where do you need to trust that God is working behind the scenes in your life?

. . . .
. . . .
. . . .

What would it look like to rest in the reliability of His Word this season?

> **PRAYER**
>
> *Father, thank You that the story of Jesus isn't fiction or fantasy—it's fact. You moved in history, and You are still moving today. Strengthen my confidence in Your Word, and help me trust that You're at work in my life—even when I can't see it yet. Amen.*

DAY EIGHTEEN
WHERE YOU BELONG

Luke 2:4-5 NIV *So Joseph also went up from the town of Nazareth in Galilee to Judea, to Bethlehem the town of David, because he belonged to the house and line of David. He went there to register with Mary, who was pledged to be married to him and was expecting a child.*

Identity is about who you are.
But belonging is about where you fit.

Joseph belonged to the house and line of David.

Most likely, he and Mary weren't traveling alone. Descendants of David would have made the same journey, creating a caravan of relatives—brothers, sisters, aunts, uncles, and family friends. Bethlehem would have been packed, overflowing with travelers returning to their ancestral homes. That's why there was "no room in the inn"—not because of a harsh innkeeper, but because homes were already filled to capacity.

Though mandated by Rome, this journey reconnected Joseph to his family roots. These were his people. His family. This was where he belonged.

The Christmas story reminds us how vital spiritual family truly is. You may not be traveling with relatives to register for a census—but you're still on a journey.

And no one is meant to walk it alone.

Real belonging happens when you walk with people who truly know you, fight for you, and love you—no matter what. That kind of connection doesn't come easily. It takes time, intentionality, and shared steps. But it's worth it. In fact, it's how God designed you.

You weren't made only to believe in God—you were made to belong to His people. To be part of a spiritual family. A church home. A place where others know your name, walk beside you in joy and sorrow, and help carry your burdens along the way.

Belonging sounds good in theory, but it's difficult to know where to begin. What if you started right here by taking a courageous step to attend a church? Show up. Fill out the card. Join a group. Start serving. Let someone know the real you.

Belonging is a journey. And it starts with a step.

REFLECTION

Are you trying to walk with God without walking with others?

. . . .

. . . .

What step can you take this week toward spiritual community?

. . . .

. . . .

What fears are holding you back from truly belonging?

. . . .

. . . .

. . . .

PRAYER

Father, thank You that I was never meant to walk through life alone. Give me courage to take the next step toward the people You've placed in my path. Help me find and embrace the spiritual family You've prepared for me. Teach me how to truly belong—and lead me every step of the way. Amen.

DAY NINETEEN
CROWDED OUT

Luke 2:6-7 NIV *While they were there, the time came for the baby to be born, and she gave birth to her firstborn, a son. She wrapped him in cloths and placed him in a manger, because there was no guest room available for them.*

The moment had come. After a long and exhausting journey to Bethlehem, Mary went into labor. But when the time came to deliver the Savior of the world, there was no guest room available.

Not exactly the royal welcome we might expect for the King of Kings.

We often imagine Mary and Joseph being turned away by a grumpy innkeeper, forced to settle for a stable. But Luke's language actually suggests something different. The word translated as "guest room" refers more to a spare room in a relative's home than a public inn. In other words, they were likely with family—but there was simply no space for them to stay in the usual quarters.

So the Son of God was laid in a manger—an animal feeding trough. No crib. No comfort. Just a humble beginning.

It wasn't because people were cruel. It was because they were full. Busy. Preoccupied. Consumed by their own responsibilities and travel needs. And in their fullness, they missed what God was doing right in front of them.

It's still easy to do the same.

We fill our days with events and errands, traditions and to-do lists, leaving little space for wonder or worship. The problem isn't that we've rejected Jesus—it's that we've crowded Him out.

What if this Christmas, we cleared some room?

What if we made space not just in our homes, but in our hearts?

REFLECTION

What's filling up your time, attention, or energy this season?

. . . .
. . . .
. . . .

Are you unintentionally crowding Jesus out?

. . . .
. . . .
. . . .

What's one way you can intentionally make room for Him today?

. . . .
. . . .
. . . .

PRAYER

Jesus, I don't want to be so full that I miss You. Forgive me for the ways I've let distractions and busyness take up space that belongs to You. This Christmas, I want to make room in my heart for Your presence. Amen.

DAY TWENTY
GOOD NEWS FOR THE UNLIKELY

Luke 2:8-9 NIV *And there were shepherds living out in the fields nearby, keeping watch over their flocks at night. An angel of the Lord appeared to them, and the glory of the Lord shone around them, and they were terrified.*

The very first people to hear the announcement of Jesus' birth weren't kings or priests. They weren't wealthy landowners or influential leaders. Instead, God chose shepherds—ordinary, overlooked workers spending another long night in the fields.

Shepherds lived on the fringes of society. They were often considered untrustworthy, commonly looked down upon, and certainly not admired. Their work was hard, dirty, and lonely. They didn't have a seat at the table of power or influence. By every cultural measure, they were unlikely candidates to receive heaven's greatest news.

But this is where the Christmas story surprises us. When God sent His angels to announce the birth of His Son, He didn't go to the temple courts or royal palaces. He lit up the night sky over a field. He entrusted the greatest news in history to people the world passed by without a second thought—shepherds.

This wasn't an accident. It was a picture of God's heart. In His kingdom, the humble are lifted, the overlooked are honored, and the unlikely are chosen. The shepherds remind us that God's love isn't reserved for the powerful or privileged—it's for everyone, especially those considered insignificant. Those unseen. Even rejected.

And there's more. The shepherds give us a glimpse of the kind of person Jesus would become. Born in Bethlehem, the city of shepherds and kings, He would later call Himself the Good Shepherd—the One who knows His sheep, calls them by name, and lays down His life for them. From the very beginning His mission was clear: to seek and save the lost, the forgotten, and the least likely.

If God announced His Son's birth to shepherds, then you can be certain He hasn't overlooked you.

REFLECTION

Where do you feel overlooked or forgotten?

. . . .
. . . .
. . . .

How does the shepherds' story encourage you to believe God sees you and chooses you, right where you are?

. . . .
. . . .
. . . .

PRAYER

Father, thank You for showing me that no one is too unlikely for Your love. Just as You announced the birth of Jesus to shepherds in the fields, remind me that You see me in the places where I feel forgotten. Help me trust that Your good news is for me, and give me courage to share it with others. Amen.

DAY TWENTY ONE
GOOD NEWS FOR EVERYONE

Luke 2:10-11 NIV *But the angel said to them, 'Do not be afraid. I bring you good news that will cause great joy for all the people. Today in the town of David a Savior has been born to you; he is the Messiah, the Lord.'*

For all the people.

Think about a wedding, a birthday party, or even dinner at your favorite restaurant. There's always a limit—space runs out, seats fill up, budgets can only stretch so far. Invitations are selective. Not everyone can come.

But the kingdom of God is different. From the very beginning of Jesus' arrival, the angel's announcement made it clear: this invitation is for everyone. No one is excluded. God's Messiah isn't just for the few, but for the many.

And yet, the joy of Christmas is not only in the wide scope of the invitation. The greater joy is found in the One who was born: "a Savior has been born to you; he is the Messiah, the Lord." Jesus came to take away the sins of the world (John 1:29). If all are invited but no salvation is offered, the news would be hollow. What makes this truly good news is that forgiveness and eternal life are found in Him.

That's why Christmas brings great joy—because the Savior has come and His salvation is for everyone. All are invited.

For all the people.

And that includes you.

REFLECTION

How does it encourage you to know that Jesus' invitation is for all people—including you?

. . . .
. . . .
. . . .

Who in your life needs to hear that truth this season?

. . . .
. . . .
. . . .

PRAYER

Lord, thank You for sending Jesus as the Savior for all people. Thank You that Your invitation includes me. Help me live in the joy of that truth and share it with others who need hope today. Amen.

DAY TWENTY TWO
SIGN OF THE MANGER

Luke 2:12 NIV *This will be a sign to you: You will find a baby wrapped in cloths and lying in a manger.*

The manger may be the most recognized detail of the Christmas story. It appears in nativity scenes, Christmas cards, and church productions across the world. But its purpose was not primarily to symbolize the messiness of our lives or the humility of Christ's entrance. The angel gave the manger a specific role: it was meant to be a sign.

Signs point us in the right direction. They inform, confirm, or warn. For the shepherds, the manger was heaven's way of removing all doubt. The Savior had come and this was how they would recognize Him. Not in a palace. Not wrapped in royal garments. But in the unexpected place of a feeding trough.

Every detail of that night was intentional. The shepherds would know exactly which baby was the Messiah: He would be wrapped in cloths and lying in a manger. It was God's way of saying, This is the One. Don't miss Him.

And the sign still speaks today. The manger isn't just part of their story—it's part of ours. We aren't searching the streets of Bethlehem to identify the Christ child. For us, the manger functions less as a sign and more as a reminder. It reminds us that God's plan is intentional, that He often works in unexpected ways, and that the Savior truly entered our world in humility. It tells us we don't have to look for Jesus in power or prestige—He delights in drawing near in surprising ways. Sometimes His greatest work begins in the most ordinary of settings.

But most importantly, the manger reminds us that Jesus is Savior, Messiah, and Lord.

God has come near.
He is with you.
And His name is Jesus.

REFLECTION

What "signs" has God placed in your life to remind you of His presence and promises?

. . . .
. . . .
. . . .

How can the simplicity of the manger help you recognize and worship Jesus in your daily life?

. . . .
. . . .
. . . .

PRAYER

Lord Jesus, thank You for coming in such a humble way, yet with such clear purpose. Help me not to miss the signs of Your presence in my life. Thank You for reminding me that You are my Savior, my Messiah, and my Lord. Amen.

DAY TWENTY THREE
HEAVEN TO EARTH

Luke 2:13-14 NIV *Suddenly a great company of the heavenly host appeared with the angel, praising God and saying, 'Glory to God in the highest heaven, and on earth peace to those on whom his favor rests.*

Imagine the scene.

The night sky, once quiet and dark, suddenly erupts. Not just one angel, but an entire company of heaven's army appears, praising God in radiant glory. The brilliance, the majesty, the breathtaking blaze of light filling the heavens—it must have left the shepherds speechless.

And that was just what they could see. Imagine what they heard.

The sound of angels declaring the praise of God. Was it song? Chant? A heavenly chorus unlike anything on earth? Our greatest Christmas hymns—Angels We Have Heard on High and Hark! The Herald Angels Sing—are only faint echoes of that moment. Words and music can point us there, but they cannot fully capture it.

And perhaps that's the point. Sometimes the right response is not to explain or even to act, but simply to stand in awe. Christmas invites us to pause and soak in the wonder. Nothing to prove. Nothing to accomplish. Just hearts open to the glory of God.

In that moment, heaven broke into earth. Peace had come—not just the absence of conflict, but the presence of God's favor resting on humanity. The glory of God had come down for us. For them. For you. For me.

What do we do with such news? We start where the shepherds did: by sitting with it. Let the majesty of God's presence and the peace of Christ settle deep in your soul.

REFLECTION

How easy is it for you to pause in the middle of a busy season and simply sit in awe of God?

. . . .
. . . .
. . . .

What would it look like this week to create space to rest in His peace and glory?

. . . .
. . . .
. . . .

PRAYER

Father, thank You for sending peace from heaven to earth through Jesus. Teach me to slow down and truly see the wonder of Your glory this Christmas. Fill my heart with awe, and let Your peace rest on me today. Amen.

DAY TWENTY FOUR
LET'S GO!

Luke 2:15–18 NIV *When the angels had left them and gone into heaven, the shepherds said to one another, 'Let's go to Bethlehem and see this thing that has happened, which the Lord has told us about.' So they hurried off and found Mary and Joseph, and the baby, who was lying in the manger. When they had seen him, they spread the word concerning what had been told them about this child, and all who heard it were amazed at what the shepherds said to them.*

The shepherds didn't treat the angels' announcement as casual information. This wasn't news to sit on or think about later. It was urgent. Compelling. Doing nothing wasn't an option. Their response was immediate: "Let's go!"

They had to see for themselves. And when they did—when they found Mary, Joseph, and the baby lying in a manger just as the angels had said—everything changed. Their quiet night in the fields turned into the greatest night in history.

But it didn't stop there. Once they encountered Jesus, they couldn't keep it to themselves. They spread the word and their testimony amazed everyone who heard it. Ordinary shepherds became the first evangelists, proclaiming that God's promise had come true.

And isn't that how we respond to anything good? We share it. A great restaurant. A powerful movie. A book that leaves a mark on us. We can't help but talk about what impacts us. How much more should that be true of Jesus—the Savior who changes everything?

The shepherds remind us of a simple truth: encountering Jesus leads to sharing Jesus. When you've truly seen Him, silence isn't possible. The good news is too good to keep to yourself.

REFLECTION

What keeps you from responding to Jesus with the urgency of the shepherds?

. . . .
. . . .
. . . .

When was the last time you felt an urgent desire to share something God has done in your life? What made it so compelling?

. . . .
. . . .
. . . .

How can you take a step this week to see Him more clearly and share Him more boldly?

. . . .
. . . .
. . . .

PRAYER

Lord, thank You for the example of the shepherds, who responded with urgency and joy. Stir my heart with the same eagerness to seek You. And once I encounter You, give me boldness to spread the good news so others may be amazed at what You have done. Amen.

DAY TWENTY FIVE
THE TREASURE OF CHRISTMAS

Luke 2:19–20 NIV *But Mary treasured up all these things and pondered them in her heart. The shepherds returned, glorifying and praising God for all the things they had heard and seen, which were just as they had been told.*

Mary had much to hold in her heart.

The angel Gabriel's announcement.
A long and difficult journey while expecting a child.
A birth in Bethlehem with no proper place to stay.
A manger for a cradle.
Shepherds arriving to confirm the miracle proclaimed by angels.

"All these things."
There was much to ponder. And much to treasure.

But the greatest treasure of all was not the extraordinary circumstances surrounding the birth. It was the child Himself.

Jesus.
Emmanuel—God with us.
The Son of the Most High.
The Savior. The Messiah. The Lord.

Mary treasured Him, and so must we. For Christmas is not just a story of the past. It is the declaration of a present reality: the King has come. And He has not only come for Mary, Joseph, or the shepherds—He has come for you.

Two thousand years later, the question remains the same: Who is Jesus to you? A distant figure in history? A seasonal tradition? Or the Savior of your soul, the Lord of your life, the treasure above all treasures?

The shepherds responded with praise.
Mary responded with trust.
And now you are invited to respond with faith.

This Christmas, don't just ponder the story. Receive the Savior. Believe the good news. Let the wonder of Christ's coming fill your heart and lead you to treasure Him above all.

Merry Christmas.

May you find in Jesus not only the meaning of this season, but the hope of eternal life.

REFLECTION

How can you treasure Christ more fully today—not just in memory of His birth, but in the reality of His presence?

PRAYER

Jesus, You are the true treasure of Christmas. I believe You are my Savior and Lord. Fill my heart with wonder and faith today, and help me treasure You above all else—this Christmas and forever. Amen.

ONE MORE INVITATION

Thank you for taking this journey with me through the story of Christmas. One of my greatest joys in life is getting to write and talk about Jesus. He has forever changed my life, and I'm eternally grateful. But the story doesn't end here—because Jesus is still changing lives. He is still moving in the hearts of men and women all over the world.

Is He moving in yours?

Like so many before you, God may be stirring in your heart even as you read this. What better moment than now to put your faith in Jesus and begin following Him! Just as the magi were guided by a star, God is guiding you to recognize the true significance of Jesus. He is Lord and Savior. But not just one we acknowledge from a distance—who Jesus is calls for a response. Action. Change. We cannot remain the same once our eyes have been opened to Him.

Do you need to respond? If so, I invite you to pray with me right here in this moment:

"Father in heaven, thank You for Your Son Jesus. I put my faith in Him today as my Lord and Savior. I'm so thankful You came to seek and save the lost. That's me—I'm lost without You. I choose to follow You today with all my heart, soul, mind, and strength. Everything I am is Yours. I love You, Lord. Amen."

If you prayed that prayer, congratulations! This is the beginning of an incredible relationship with God. If you don't have a church, I encourage you to find one and begin walking this journey of faith with others. God never designed us to do this alone.

As you move forward, remember this: Christmas doesn't end on December 25th. The Savior who arrived in Bethlehem walks with you into every ordinary day. Treasure Him, follow Him, and let His peace, love, and hope guide your steps.

Merry Christmas—and may you carry its joy with you every single day.

With gratitude and joy,

-Andy

ABOUT THE AUTHOR
ANDREW KING

Andrew King is a pastor, writer, and communicator passionate about helping people slow down, experience Scripture, and follow Jesus with their whole lives. He serves as the Lead Pastor of HighPoint Church in Kennesaw, Georgia, where he and his wife Amy are raising their 4 children and helping others experience a real, life-changing relationship with God.

Whether preaching, teaching, or writing, Andy's heart is to point people to the hope of the gospel. *The Christmas Collection* is his first devotional book, written to help readers experience the joy and wonder of Christ in the middle of a busy season.

When Andy isn't writing or pastoring, you can find him cheering on the St. Louis Cardinals, building LEGOs as a hobby, or enjoying a piping hot cup of coffee.

You can connect with Andrew and learn more about his ministry at:

https://linktr.ee/andrewmorganking

www.ingramcontent.com/pod-product-compliance
Lightning Source LLC
Chambersburg PA
CBHW030448100526
44580CB00002B/33